PRO HOCKEY RECORDS

A GUIDE FOR EVERY FAN

BY SHANE FREDERICK

COMPASS POINT BOOKS
a capstone imprint

Compass Point Books are published by Capstone
1710 Roe Crest Drive, North Mankato, Minnesota 56003
www.mycapstone.com

Editorial Credits

Lauren Dupuis-Perez, editor; Sara Radka, designer;
Eric Gohl, media researcher; Laura Manthe, production specialist

Library of Congress Cataloging-in-Publication Data

Library of Congress Cataloging-in-Publication data is available on the Library of Congress website.

ISBN 978-1-5435-5462-5 (library binding)
ISBN 978-1-5435-5934-7 (paperback)
ISBN 978-1-5435-5467-0 (eBook PDF)

Photo Credits

Getty Images: Allsport/Al Bello, 53 (top), Allsport/Elsa, 49 (top), Allsport/Glenn Cratty, 24 (top), Allsport/Ian Tomlinson, 11 (bottom), Barry Gossage, 58 (bottom), Bruce Bennett, 4, Claus Andersen, 56 (left), Dave Sandford, 12, Design Pics/Con Tanasiuk, 22 (bottom), Gregory Shamus, 56 (right), iStockphoto/sbayram, background, Jason Halstead, 15 (top), Jim McIsaac, 60, Joel Auerbach, 17 (bottom), Mike Powell, 38, NHLI/Dave Sandford, 7 (top), NHLI/Rick Stewart, 8 (top), Patrick McDermott, 6, razihusin, 21, Rick Stewart, 16, 26, 31, 55, Tim Smith, 18; Newscom: David Abel, 17 (top), Icon SMI/Cliff Welsh, 33 (bottom), Icon SMI/IHA, 19, 28 (bottom), 57 (bottom), 57 (top), Icon SMI/IHA/Robert Beck, 52 (bottom), Icon SMI/John Cordes, 53 (bottom), Icon SMI/John McDonough, 7 (bottom), Icon SMI/Steven King, 23, iPhoto.ca/Larry MacDougal, 46, KRT/Jerry Lodriguss, 52 (top), QMI Agency/Edmonton Sun/Perry Mah, 43 (bottom), ZUMAPRESS/Bildbryan, 11 (top), 15 (bottom), 29, 41, 50 (bottom), 50 (top), ZUMAPRESS/Philadelphia Inquirer, 51 (top), ZUMAPRESS/SCG/Bob Fina, 44, ZUMAPRESS/The Toronto Star, 8 (bottom), ZUMAPRESS/The Toronto Star/Doug Griffin, 21 (top) ; Shutterstock: klarka0608, 49 (bottom), Longchalerm Rungruang, cover (hockey equipment), Shooter Bob Square Lenses, cover (ice); Wikimedia: Benjamin Reed, 32, Conrad Poirier, 45 (top), Håkan Dahlström, 14, 20, j_rho, 27 (bottom), JamesTeterenko, 48, Jim Tyron, 35, kcxd, 27 (top), Keith Allison Photo, 40, Michael Miller, 36, 47, 54, Montreal Canadiens, 33 (top), NHL/Chicago Blackhawks, 24 (bottom), NHL/New York Islanders, 43 (top), NHL/St. Louis Blues, 30, Paul Darling, 45 (bottom), Ralston-Purina Company, 58 (top), Resolute, 10, Rick Dikeman, 28 (top), Sarah Connors, 51 (bottom)

All stats are through the 2017–18 NHL season and 2018 playoffs. Pre-NHL statistics are not included.

Printed in the United States of America.
012019   000061

Table of Contents

RECORDS FROM THE ICE

In his second and third seasons as a National Hockey League (NHL) player, Connor McDavid of the Edmonton Oilers led the league in scoring. He racked up 100 points (30 goals, 70 assists) in 2016–17 and 108 points (41 goals, 67 assists) in 2017–18. Those weren't record-setting performances. However, McDavid did have two scoring championships by the age of 21. Only one other player in NHL history had accomplished this feat.

That player was another young Oilers star, one who Edmonton fans are reminded of when they watch McDavid play: the "Great One," Wayne Gretzky.

McDavid had an impressive start to his career, but he has a long way to go to match more of what Gretzky did. Gretzky holds many NHL records, and he put some of them far, far out of reach of any other player. No one has scored more points, goals, or assists than Gretzky, whether over a career or over a single season. In fact, if you took away Gretzky's goals, his career assist total would still be enough to make him the NHL's all-time points leader. Perhaps McDavid will be the one to eclipse that stat and set a new record.

Setting a record is a big deal. It's a historic event. It establishes a player as one of the greats of his or her sport. It's a measuring stick for young and future players. When it comes to points, McDavid, Sidney Crosby, Alex Ovechkin, Patrick Kane, and others are all chasing Gretzky, just as Mario Lemieux, Steve Yzerman, and Teemu Selänne did before—and just as Gretzky did with Gordie Howe.

Gretzky doesn't have all of the NHL records. There are high marks for defensemen and goaltenders, coaches and enforcers, winners and, yes, even losers.

What do you think are the greatest records in hockey history? Do they belong to Gretzky? To Martin Brodeur? To Glenn Hall? To the Montreal Canadiens?

Not sure? This book has them all. Read on—you're bound to find your favorite.

CHAPTER 1

Skater Records

Late in the 2017–18 season, Washington Capitals forward Alex Ovechkin scored his 600th career goal. It was a milestone passed by just 19 other players in NHL history. Ovechkin was the fourth-fastest player to reach 600. However, reaching Wayne Gretzky's record of 894 goals will be a much more difficult task.

Many players have come and gone, trying to catch the Great Gretzky or even Gordie Howe, whose 801 goals were once the standard. Even if they didn't quite reach the all-time record, Jaromír Jágr, Mark Messier, and Brett Hull still rank among the greatest goal scorers in hockey history. So does Ovechkin, who, earlier during the 2017–18 season, set a record of his own for career overtime goals.

The great players are often defined by the records they set or come close to setting, whether it's over a career, a season, or even a single game.

Most Points

SINGLE SEASON				
1	**Wayne Gretzky**	215	Oilers	1985–86
2	**Wayne Gretzky**	212	Oilers	1981–82
3	**Wayne Gretzky**	208	Oilers	1984–85
4	**Wayne Gretzky**	205	Oilers	1983–84
5	**Mario Lemieux**	199	Penguins	1988–89
6	**Wayne Gretzky**	196	Oilers	1982–83
7	**Wayne Gretzky**	183	Oilers	1986–87
8	**Mario Lemieux**	168	Penguins	1987–88
9	**Wayne Gretzky**	168	Kings	1988–89
10	**Wayne Gretzky**	164	Oilers	1980–81

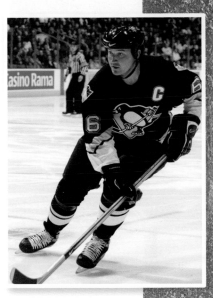

▲ Mario Lemieux

WORLD HOCKEY ASSOCIATION

Wayne Gretzky also scored 110 points (46 goals, 64 assists) in the World Hockey Association (WHA). The WHA was a rival league of the NHL's from 1972 to 1979. Gretzky played one year in the WHA before his Oilers merged into the NHL. Gordie Howe played six seasons in the WHA after a long career with the Red Wings. He scored 508 points (174 goals, 334 assists) for the Houston Aeros and the New England Whalers.

Most Points

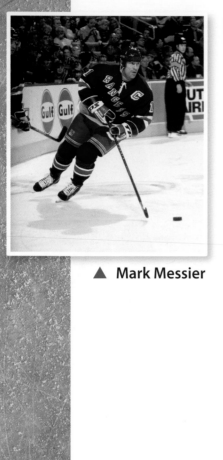

▲ Mark Messier

CAREER

1	Wayne Gretzky	2,857	Oilers/Kings/Blues/Rangers	1979–1999
2	Jaromír Jágr	1,921	Penguins/Capitals/Rangers/Flyers/Stars/Bruins/Devils/Panthers/Flames	1990–2008, 2011–2018
3	Mark Messier	1,887	Oilers/Rangers/Canucks	1979–2004
4	Gordie Howe	1,850	Red Wings/Whalers	1946–1971, 1979–1980
5	Ron Francis	1,798	Whalers/Penguins/Hurricanes/Maple Leafs	1981–2004
6	Marcel Dionne	1,771	Red Wings/Kings/Rangers	1971–1989
7	Steve Yzerman	1,755	Red Wings	1983–2006
8	Mario Lemieux	1,723	Penguins	1984–1994, 1995–1997, 2000–2004, 2005–2006
9	Joe Sakic	1,641	Nordiques/Avalanche	1988–2009
10	Phil Esposito	1,590	Blackhawks/Bruins/Rangers	1963–1981

POINTS ALL AROUND

Darryl Sittler of the Maple Leafs holds the record for most points in a game, with 10 on a night in 1976. He scored six goals and assisted on four others in an 11-4 victory over the Bruins. The record for points in a single period is six, set by the Islanders' Bryan Trottier in 1978.

Goals

SINGLE SEASON

1	Wayne Gretzky	92	Oilers	1981–82
2	Wayne Gretzky	87	Oilers	1983–84
3	Brett Hull	86	Blues	1990–91
4	Mario Lemieux	85	Penguins	1988–89
5	Phil Esposito	76	Bruins	1970–71
	Alexander Mogilny	76	Sabres	1992–93
	Teemu Selänne	76	Jets	1992–93
8	Wayne Gretzky	73	Oilers	1984–85
9	Brett Hull	72	Blues	1989–90
10	Wayne Gretzky	71	Oilers	1982–83
	Jari Kurri	71	Oilers	1984–85

CAREER

1	Wayne Gretzky	894	Oilers/Kings/Blues/Rangers	1979–1999
2	Gordie Howe	801	Red Wings/Whalers	1946–1971, 1979–1980
3	Jaromír Jágr	766	Penguins/Capitals/Rangers/Flyers/Stars/Bruins/Devils/Panthers/Flames	1990–2008, 2011–2018
4	Brett Hull	741	Flames/Blues/Stars/Red Wings/Coyotes	1986–2006
5	Marcel Dionne	731	Red Wings/Kings/Rangers	1971–1989
6	Phil Esposito	717	Blackhawks/Bruins/Rangers	1963–1981
7	Mike Gartner	708	Capitals/North Stars/Rangers/Maple Leafs/Coyotes	1979–1998
8	Mark Messier	694	Oilers/Rangers/Canucks	1979–2004
9	Steve Yzerman	692	Red Wings	1983–2006
10	Mario Lemieux	690	Penguins	1984–1994, 1995–1997, 2000–2004, 2005–2006

Power-Play Goals

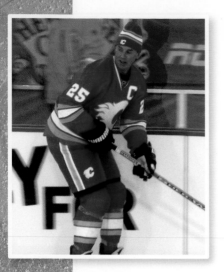

▲ Joe Nieuwendyk

SINGLE SEASON

1	Tim Kerr	34	Flyers	1985–86
2	Dave Andreychuk	32	Sabres/Maple Leafs	1992–93
3	Joe Nieuwendyk	31	Flames	1987–88
	Mario Lemieux	31	Penguins	1988–89
	Mario Lemieux	31	Penguins	1995–96
6	Michel Goulet	29	Nordiques	1987–88
	Brett Hull	29	Blues	1990–91
	Brett Hull	29	Blues	1992–93
9	Mike Bossy	28	Islanders	1980–81
	Michel Goulet	28	Nordiques	1985–86
	Dave Andreychuk	28	Sabres	1991–92

CAREER

1	Dave Andreychuk	274	Sabres/Maple Leafs/Devils/Bruins/Avalanche/Lightning	1982–2006
2	Brett Hull	265	Flames/Blues/Stars/Red Wings/Coyotes	1986–2006
3	Teemu Selänne	255	Jets/Ducks/Sharks/Avalanche	1992–2014
4	Luc Robitaille	247	Kings/Penguins/Rangers/Red Wings	1986–2006
	Phil Esposito	246	Blackhawks/Bruins/Rangers	1963–1981
6	Brendan Shanahan	237	Devils/Blues/Whalers/Red Wings/Rangers	1987–2009
7	Mario Lemieux	236	Penguins	1984–1994, 1995–1997, 2000–2004, 2005–2006
8	Marcel Dionne	234	Red Wings/Kings/Rangers	1971–1989
9	Dino Ciccarelli	232	North Stars/Capitals/Red Wings/Lightning/Panthers	1980–1999
10	Alex Ovechkin	229	Capitals	2005–2018*

active player

Short-Handed Goals

1	**Mario Lemieux**	13	Penguins	1988–89
2	**Wayne Gretzky**	12	Oilers	1983–84
3	**Wayne Gretzky**	11	Oilers	1984–85
4	**Marcel Dionne**	10	Red Wings	1974–75
	Mario Lemieux	10	Penguins	1987–88
	Dirk Graham	10	Blackhawks	1988–89
7	**Kent Nilsson**	9	Flames	1983–84
	Paul Coffey	9	Oilers	1985–86
	Brian Rolston	9	Bruins	2001–02
10	**14 players tied with 8**			

▲ Kent Nilsson

SHORT-HANDED GOALS

A team is short-handed when one of its players is in the penalty box, putting the other team on the power play. Despite having fewer players, the short-handed team still has the opportunity to score. Theoren Fleury of the Flames holds the record for short-handed goals in a single game. He scored three goals—a hat trick—against the Blues' power play during a game in 1991.

Short-Handed Goals

CAREER

1	**Wayne Gretzky**	73	Oilers/Kings/Blues/Rangers	1979–1999
2	**Mark Messier**	63	Oilers/Rangers/Canucks	1979–2004
3	**Steve Yzerman**	50	Red Wings	1983–2006
4	**Mario Lemieux**	49	Penguins	1984–1994, 1995–1997, 2000–2004, 2005–2006
5	**Butch Goring**	39	Kings/Islanders/Bruins	1969–1985
	Jari Kurri	39	Oilers/Kings/Rangers/Ducks/Avalanche	1980–1998
	Dave Poulin	39	Flyers/Bruins/Capitals	1982–1995
8	**Sergei Fedorov**	36	Red Wings/Ducks/Blue Jackets/Capitals	1990–2009
9	**Dirk Graham**	35	North Stars/Blackhawks	1983–1995
	Theoren Fleury	35	Flames/Avalanche/Rangers/Blackhawks	1988–2003

▲ Steve Yzerman

Overtime Goals

CAREER

1	**Alex Ovechkin**	22	Capitals	2005–2018*
2	**Jaromír Jágr**	19	Penguins/Capitals/Rangers/Flyers/Stars/Bruins/Devils/Panthers/Flames	1990–2008, 2011–2018
3	**Patrik Elias**	16	Devils	1995–2016
	Daniel Sedin	16	Canucks	2000–2018
5	**Sergei Fedorov**	15	Red Wings/Ducks/Blue Jackets/Capitals	1990–2009
	Mats Sundin	15	Nordiques/Maple Leafs/Canucks	1990–2009
	Marian Hossa	15	Senators/Thrashers/Penguins/Red Wings/Blackhawks	1997–2017
8	**Ilya Kovalchuk**	14	Thrashers/Devils	2001–2013
	Five players tied with 13			

* active player

Game-Winning Goals

SINGLE SEASON

1	Phil Esposito	16	Bruins	1970–71
	Phil Esposito	16	Bruins	1971–72
	Michel Goulet	16	Nordiques	1983–84
4	Cooney Weiland	14	Bruins	1929–30
	Pavel Bure	14	Panthers	1990–2000
6	Charlie Conacher	13	Maple Leafs	1934–35
	Guy Lafleur	13	Canadiens	1978–79
	Jari Kurri	13	Oilers	1984–85
	Jeremy Roenick	13	Blackhawks	1991–92
	Cam Neely	13	Bruins	1993–94
	Peter Bondra	13	Capitals	1997–98

CAREER

1	Jaromír Jágr	135	Penguins/Capitals/Rangers/Flyers/Stars/Bruins/Devils/Panthers/Flames	1990–2008, 2011–2018
2	Gordie Howe	121	Red Wings/Whalers	1946–1971, 1979–1980
3	Phil Esposito	118	Blackhawks/Bruins/Rangers	1963–1981
4	Brett Hull	110	Flames/Blues/Stars/Red Wings/Coyotes	1986–2006
	Teemu Selänne	110	Jets/Ducks/Sharks/Avalanche	1992–2014
6	Brendan Shanahan	109	Devils/Blues/Whalers/Red Wings/Rangers	1987–2009
7	Patrick Marleau	103	Sharks/Maple Leafs	1997–2018*
8	Alex Ovechkin	102	Capitals	2005–2018*
9	Jarome Iginla	101	Flames/Penguins/Bruins/Avalanche/Kings	1996–2017
10	Bobby Hull	98	Blackhawks/Jets/Whalers	1957–1972, 1979–1980
	Guy Lafleur	98	Canadiens/Rangers/Nordiques	1971–1985, 1988–1991

active player

RECORD FACT

A game-winning goal is any goal that gives a team one more goal than the opponent finished with—the third goal in a 4-2 win, for example. Over his long career, Jaromír Jágr had a knack for scoring game-winners. Jágr broke Gordie Howe's record in 2013 while playing for the Devils, one of nine teams he played for.

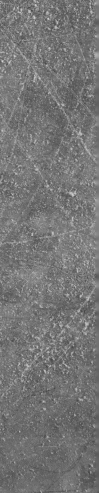

Penalty Shot Goals

	CAREER			
1	**Pavel Bure**	7	Canucks/Panthers/Rangers	1991–2003
2	**Mario Lemieux**	6	Penguins	1984–1994, 1995–1997, 2000–2004, 2005–2006
3	**Vincent Lecavalier**	5	Lightning	1998–2018*
4	**Charlie Conacher**	4	Maple Leafs/Red Wings/American	1929–1941
	Joe Sakic	4	Nordiques/Avalanche	1988–2009
	Mats Sundin	4	Nordiques/Maple Leafs/Canucks	1990–2009
	David Vyborny	4	Blue Jackets	2000–2008
	Brad Marchand	4	Bruins	2009–2018*

active player

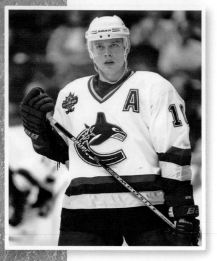

▲ Pavel Bure

Hat Tricks

	CAREER			
1	**Wayne Gretzky**	50	Oilers/Kings/Blues/Rangers	1979–1999
2	**Mario Lemieux**	40	Penguins	1984–1994, 1995–1997, 2000–2004, 2005–2006
3	**Mike Bossy**	39	Islanders	1977–1987
4	**Brett Hull**	33	Flames/Blues/Stars/Red Wings/Coyotes	1986–2006
5	**Phil Esposito**	32	Blackhawks/Bruins/Rangers	1963–1981
	Bobby Hull	28	Blackhawks/Jets/Whalers	1957–1980
7	**Marcel Dionne**	28	Red Wings/Kings/Rangers	1971–1989
8	**Maurice Richard**	26	Canadiens	1942–1960
9	**Cy Denneny**	25	Senators/Bruins	1917–1929
10	**Jari Kurri**	23	Oilers/Kings/Rangers/Ducks/Avalanche	1980–1998

RECORD FACT

A player earns a hat track by scoring three goals in a single game. Wayne Gretzky holds the single-season record for hat tricks, with 10. In fact, he racked up 10 hat tricks in a season twice (1981–82 and 1983–84). Mario Lemieux and Mike Bossy each had a nine-hat-trick season.

Goals in Rookie Season

SINGLE SEASON

1	Teemu Selänne	76	Jets	1992–93
2	Mike Bossy	53	Islanders	1977–78
3	Alex Ovechkin	52	Capitals	2005–06
4	Joe Nieuwendyk	51	Flames	1987–88
5	Dale Hawerchuk	45	Jets	1981–82
	Luc Robitaille	45	Kings	1986–87
7	Rick Martin	44	Sabres	1971–72
	Barry Pederson	44	Bruins	1981–82
9	Steve Larmer	43	Blackhawks	1982–83
	Mario Lemieux	43	Penguins	1984–85

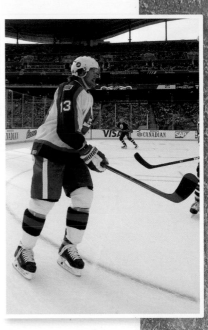

▲ Teemu Selänne

Points in Rookie Season

SINGLE SEASON

1	Teemu Selänne	132	Jets	1992–93
2	Peter Stastny	109	Nordiques	1980–81
3	Alex Ovechkin	106	Capitals	2005–06
4	Dale Hawerchuk	103	Jets	1981–82
5	Joe Juneau	102	Bruins	1992–93
	Sidney Crosby	102	Penguins	2005–06
7	Mario Lemieux	100	Penguins	1984–85
8	Neal Broten	98	North Stars	1981–82
9	Bryan Trottier	95	Islanders	1975–76
10	Barry Pederson	92	Bruins	1981–82
	Joe Nieuwendyk	92	Flames	1987–88

▲ Bryan Trottier

Assists

SINGLE SEASON				
1	**Wayne Gretzky**	163	Oilers	1985–86
2	**Wayne Gretzky**	135	Oilers	1984–86
3	**Wayne Gretzky**	125	Oilers	1982–83
4	**Wayne Gretzky**	122	Kings	1990–91
5	**Wayne Gretzky**	121	Oilers	1986–87
6	**Wayne Gretzky**	120	Oilers	1981–82
7	**Wayne Gretzky**	118	Oilers	1983–84
8	**Wayne Gretzky**	114	Kings	1988–89
	Mario Lemieux	114	Penguins	1988–89
10	**Wayne Gretzky**	109	Oilers	1980–81
	Wayne Gretzky	109	Oilers	1987–88

ASSIST MANIA

Who holds the record for the most assists in one game? Wayne Gretzky, of course. Three times in his career with the Oilers—in 1980, 1985, and 1986—he assisted on seven goals in a game. The only other player to accomplish that feat was the Red Wings' Billy Taylor, who did it first in 1947. The record for most assists in one period is five, set by the Jets' Dale Hawerchuk in 1984.

▲ **Wayne Gretzky**

CAREER

1	**Wayne Gretzky**	1,963	Oilers/Kings/Blues/Rangers	1979–1999
2	**Ron Francis**	1,249	Whalers/Penguins/Hurricanes/Maple Leafs	1981–2004
3	**Mark Messier**	1,193	Oilers/Rangers/Canucks	1979–2004
4	**Ray Bourque**	1,169	Bruins/Avalanche	1979–2001
5	**Jaromír Jágr**	1,155	Penguins/Capitals/Rangers/Flyers/Stars/Bruins/Devils/Panthers/Flames	1990–2008, 2011–2018
6	**Paul Coffey**	1,135	Oilers/Penguins/Kings/Red Wings/Whalers/Flyers/Blackhawks/Hurricanes/Bruins	1980–2001
7	**Adam Oates**	1,079	Red Wings/Blues/Bruins/Capitals/Flyers/Ducks/Oilers	1985–2004
8	**Steve Yzerman**	1,063	Red Wings	1983–2006
9	**Gordie Howe**	1,049	Red Wings/Whalers	1946–1971, 1979–1980
10	**Marcel Dionne**	1,040	Red Wings/Kings/Rangers	1971–1989

▲ Ron Francis

▲ Jaromír Jágr

RECORD FACT

Sometimes it's the goaltenders who get the offensive rush started. If a goal-scoring play works out right, a goalie will get an assist. Tom Barrasso, who played from 1983 to 2003, helped out on more goals than any other goalie. He finished his career with 48 assists.

Points by Defensemen

▲ Paul Coffey

SINGLE SEASON

1	Bobby Orr	139	Bruins	1970–71
2	Paul Coffey	138	Oilers	1985–86
3	Bobby Orr	135	Bruins	1974–75
4	Paul Coffey	126	Oilers	1983–84
5	Bobby Orr	122	Bruins	1973–74
6	Paul Coffey	121	Oilers	1984–85
7	Bobby Orr	120	Bruins	1969–70
8	Bobby Orr	117	Bruins	1971–72
9	Paul Coffey	113	Penguins	1988–89
10	Paul Coffey	103	Penguins	1989–90
	Al MacInnis	103	Flames	1990–91

CAREER

1	Ray Bourque	1,579	Bruins/Avalanche	1979–2001
2	Paul Coffey	1,531	Oilers/Penguins/Kings/Red Wings/Whalers/Flyers/Blackhawks/Hurricanes/Bruins	1980–2001
3	Al MacInnis	1,274	Flames/Blues	1981–2004
4	Phil Housley	1,232	Sabres/Jets/Blues/Flames/Devils/Capitals/Blackhawks/Maple Leafs	1982–2003
5	Larry Murphy	1,217	Kings/Capitals/North Stars/Penguins/Maple Leafs/Red Wings	1980–2001
6	Nicklas Lidstrom	1,142	Red Wings	1991–2012
7	Denis Potvin	1,052	Islanders	1973–1988
8	Brian Leetch	1,028	Rangers/Maple Leafs/Bruins	1987–2006
9	Larry Robinson	958	Canadiens/Kings	1972–1992
10	Chris Chelios	948	Canadiens/Blackhawks/Red Wings/Thrashers	1983–2010

RECORD FACT

The Maple Leafs' Ian Turnbull was the only defenseman in NHL history to score five goals in a game. He accomplished the feat in 1977. Eight defensemen, including Turnbull in 1981, have had four-goal games.

Goals by Defensemen

1	**Paul Coffey**	48	Oilers	1985–86
2	**Bobby Orr**	46	Bruins	1974–75
3	**Paul Coffey**	40	Oilers	1983–84
4	**Doug Wilson**	39	Blackhawks	1981–82
5	**Bobby Orr**	37	Bruins	1970–71
	Bobby Orr	37	Bruins	1971–72
	Paul Coffey	37	Oilers	1984–85
8	**Kevin Hatcher**	34	Capitals	1992–93
9	**Bobby Orr**	33	Bruins	1969–70
10	**Bobby Orr**	32	Bruins	1973–74

▲ Bobby Orr

CAREER

1	**Ray Bourque**	410	Bruins/Avalanche	1979–2001
2	**Paul Coffey**	396	Oilers/Penguins/Kings/ Red Wings/Whalers/ Flyers/Blackhawks/ Hurricanes/Bruins	1980–2001
3	**Al MacInnis**	340	Flames/Blues	1981–2004
4	**Phil Housley**	338	Sabres/Jets/Blues/ Flames/Devils/Capitals/ Blackhawks/Maple Leafs	1982–2003
5	**Denis Potvin**	310	Islanders	1973–1988
6	**Larry Murphy**	288	Kings/Capitals/North Stars/Penguins/Maple Leafs/Red Wings	1980–2001
7	**Red Kelly**	281	Red Wings/Maple Leafs	1947–1967
8	**Bobby Orr**	270	Bruins/Blackhawks	1966–1979
9	**Nicklas Lidstrom**	264	Red Wings	1991–2012
10	**Brian Leetch**	247	Rangers/Maple Leafs/Bruins	1987–2006

RECORD FACT

Defenseman Ray Bourque holds the NHL record for most shots on goal for a career. During his 21 seasons, the Bruins star put 6,209 shots on net.

Assists by Defensemen

SINGLE SEASON

1	**Bobby Orr**	102	Bruins	1970–71
2	**Bobby Orr**	90	Bruins	1973–74
	Paul Coffey	90	Oilers	1985–86
4	**Bobby Orr**	89	Bruins	1974–75
5	**Bobby Orr**	87	Bruins	1969–70
6	**Paul Coffey**	86	Oilers	1983–84
7	**Paul Coffey**	84	Oilers	1984–85
8	**Paul Coffey**	83	Penguins	1988–89
9	**Bobby Orr**	80	Bruins	1971–72
	Brian Leetch	80	Rangers	1991–92

▲ Brian Leetch

CAREER

1	**Ray Bourque**	1,169	Bruins/Avalanche	1979–2001
2	**Paul Coffey**	1,135	Oilers/Penguins/Kings/Red Wings/Whalers/Flyers/Blackhawks/Hurricanes/Bruins	1980–2001
3	**Al MacInnis**	934	Flames/Blues	1981–2004
4	**Larry Murphy**	929	Kings/Capitals/North Stars/Penguins/Maple Leafs/Red Wings	1980–2001
5	**Phil Housley**	894	Sabres/Jets/Blues/Flames/Devils/Capitals/Blackhawks/Maple Leafs	1982–2003
6	**Nicklas Lidstrom**	878	Red Wings	1991–2012
7	**Brian Leetch**	781	Rangers/Maple Leafs/Bruins	1987–2006
8	**Chris Chelios**	763	Canadiens/Blackhawks/Red Wings/Thrashers	1983–2010
9	**Larry Robinson**	750	Canadiens/Kings	1972–1992
10	**Denis Potvin**	742	Islanders	1973–1988

RECORD FACT

Six defensemen have had six assists in a single game. The list includes high-scoring legends Bobby Orr and Paul Coffey. The others were Babe Pratt, Pat Stapleton, Ron Stackhouse, and Gary Suter.

Plus·Minus

1	Bobby Orr	+124	Bruins	1970–71
2	Larry Robinson	+120	Canadiens	1976–77
3	Wayne Gretzky	+100	Oilers	1984–85
4	Dallas Smith	+98	Bruins	1970–71
5	Guy Lafleur	+89	Canadiens	1976–77
	Steve Shutt	+89	Canadiens	1976–77
7	Mark Howe	+87	Flyers	1985–86
8	Brad McCrimmon	+86	Flyers	1985–86
9	Bobby Orr	+84	Bruins	1973–74
10	Bobby Orr	+83	Bruins	1971–72
	Bobby Clarke	+83	Flyers	1975–76

▲ Guy Lafleur

PLUS-MINUS

A player's plus-minus record shows how the team performed while that player was on the ice. He earns a point (+1) if his team scores an even-strength or short-handed goal. He loses a point (-1) if the other team scores. Power-play and penalty-shot goals are not included in the calculation. If a player is on the ice for one of his team's goals and two of the opponents' goals, his plus-minus would be -1.

Plus-Minus

CAREER				
1	**Larry Robinson**	+722	Canadiens/Kings	1972–1992
2	**Bobby Orr**	+582	Bruins/Blackhawks	1966–1979
3	**Ray Bourque**	+527	Bruins/Avalanche	1979–2001
4	**Wayne Gretzky**	+520	Oilers/Kings/Blues/Rangers	1979–1999
5	**Bobby Clarke**	+507	Flyers	1969–1984
6	**Serge Savard**	+462	Canadiens/Jets	1966–1983
7	**Denis Potvin**	+456	Islanders	1973–1988
8	**Nicklas Lidstrom**	+450	Red Wings	1991–2012
9	**Bryan Trottier**	+449	Islanders/Penguins	1975–1994
10	**Brad McCrimmon**	+448	Bruins/Flyers/Flames/Red Wings/Whalers/Coyotes	1979–1997

POINTS PLUS

The Flyers' Tom Bladon set two records on a magical night in 1977. He set the mark for points in a game by a defenseman, with eight (four goals and four assists). This record was later matched by the Oilers' Paul Coffey. Bladon also made NHL history by finishing the 11-1 victory at +10.

Penalty Minutes

SINGLE SEASON

1	Dave Schultz	472	Flyers	1974–75
2	Paul Baxter	409	Penguins	1981–82
3	Mike Peluso	408	Blackhawks	1991–92
4	Dave Schultz	405	Kings/Penguins	1977–78
5	Marty McSorley	399	Kings	1992–93
6	Bob Probert	398	Red Wings	1987–88
7	Basil McRae	382	North Stars	1987–88
8	Joey Kocur	377	Red Wings	1985–86
9	Tim Hunter	375	Flames	1988–89
10	Donald Brashear	372	Canucks	1997–98

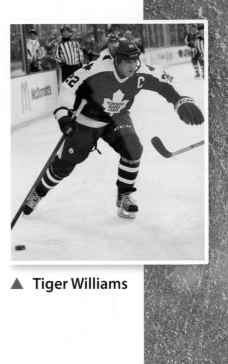

▲ Tiger Williams

CAREER

1	Tiger Williams	3,971	Maple Leafs/Canucks/Red Wings/Kings/Whalers	1974–1988
2	Dale Hunter	3,565	Nordiques/Capitals/Avalanche	1980–1999
3	Tie Domi	3,515	Maple Leafs/Rangers/Jets	1989–2006
4	Marty McSorley	3,381	Penguins/Oilers/Kings/Rangers/Sharks/Bruins	1983–2000
5	Bob Probert	3,300	Red Wings/Blackhawks	1985–2002
6	Rob Ray	3,207	Sabres/Senators	1989–2004
7	Craig Berube	3,149	Flyers/Maple Leafs/Flames/Capitals/Islanders	1986–2003
8	Tim Hunter	3,146	Flames/Nordiques/Canucks/Sharks	1981–1997
9	Chris Nilan	3,043	Canadiens/Rangers/Bruins	1979–1992
10	Rick Tocchet	2,970	Flyers/Penguins/Kings/Bruins/Capitals/Coyotes	1984–2002

RECORD FACT

Goaltenders aren't called for many penalties, but once in a while they get caught breaking the rules. Goalies don't have to sit in the penalty box, though. A teammate must sit there in his place. Ron Hextall holds the record for most penalty minutes by a goalie, compiling 584 over his career.

Seasons Played

▲ Chris Chelios

	CAREER			
1	**Gordie Howe**	26	Red Wings/Whalers	1946–1971, 1979–1980
	Chris Chelios	26	Canadiens/Blackhawks/ Red Wings/Thrashers	1983–2010
3	**Mark Messier**	25	Oilers/Rangers/Canucks	1979–2004
4	**Tim Horton**	24	Maple Leafs/Rangers/ Penguins/Sabres	1949–1974
	Alex Delvecchio	24	Red Wings	1950–1974
	Jaromír Jágr	24	Penguins/Capitals/Rangers/ Flyers/Stars/Bruins/ Devils/Panthers/Flames	1990–2008, 2011–2018

BOXED IN

Penalties are measured by minutes. Minor penalties get you two minutes in the penalty box. A major is worth five minutes, and a misconduct is worth 10 minutes. Chris Nilan of the Bruins spent more time in the box than on the ice during a game in 1991. The man with the nickname "Knuckles" was penalized a record 10 times for 42 minutes during the game. He was called for six minor penalties, two majors, a misconduct, and a game misconduct. Another NHL tough guy, the Kings' Randy Holt, received nine penalties for a record 67 penalty minutes during a game in 1979.

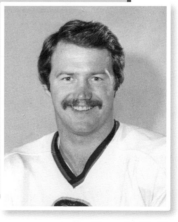

▲ Randy Holt

Games Played

1	**Gordie Howe**	1,767	Red Wings/Whalers	1946–1971, 1979–1980
2	**Mark Messier**	1,756	Oilers/Rangers/Canucks	1979–2004
3	**Jaromír Jágr**	1,733	Penguins/Capitals/Rangers/ Flyers/Stars/Bruins/ Devils/Panthers/Flames	1990–2008, 2011–2018
4	**Ron Francis**	1,731	Whalers/Penguins/ Hurricanes/Maple Leafs	1981–2004
5	**Mark Recchi**	1,652	Penguins/Flyers/Canadiens/ Hurricanes/Thrashers/ Lightning/Bruins	1988–2011
6	**Chris Chelios**	1,651	Canadiens/Blackhawks/ Red Wings/Thrashers	1983–2010
7	**Dave Andreychuk**	1,639	Sabres/Maple Leafs/Devils/ Bruins/Avalanche/Lightning	1982–2006
8	**Scott Stevens**	1,635	Capitals/Blues/Devils	1982–2004
9	**Larry Murphy**	1,615	Kings/Capitals/North Stars/Penguins/Maple Leafs/Red Wings	1980–2001
10	**Ray Bourque**	1,612	Bruins/Avalanche	1979–2001

RECORD FACT

Gordie Howe holds the record for most games played with one franchise. He played in 1,687 games for the Detroit Red Wings. Mark Messier has the record for most games, including playoff games, with 1,992.

RECORD FACT

Mike Sillinger was the NHL's ultimate journeyman. From 1990 to 2009 he played for 12 different franchises: Red Wings, Ducks, Canucks, Flyers, Lightning, Panthers, Senators, Blue Jackets, Coyotes, Blues, Predators, and Islanders. Twelve players are tied for second, playing with 10 teams during their careers.

CHAPTER 2

Goaltending Records

During the 2006–07 season, goaltender Martin Brodeur of the New Jersey Devils won 48 games. This broke a 33-year-old record. It was one of many records the longtime netminder would set over the course of his long career. Some thought it would take another three decades for that record to be equaled or passed.

Nine years later, however, the Washington Capitals' Braden Holtby put himself right into the record books. He stunned hockey fans by winning 48 games himself, tying Brodeur's impressive number.

Just like their position on the ice is different from that of other players, goaltenders get their own categories in the record books. Wins, losses, shutouts, saves, and goals allowed are just some of the statistics that can make or break goalies' careers, seasons, and games.

Martin Brodeur, Patrick Roy, and Dominik Hašek hold high spots on many lists. But they shouldn't get too comfortable. Holtby, Marc-André Fleury, and Tuukka Rask are moving on up.

Goalie Wins

SINGLE SEASON

1	Martin Brodeur	48	Devils	2006–07
2	Braden Holtby	48	Capitals	2015–16
3	Bernie Parent	47	Flyers	1973–74
	Roberto Luongo	47	Canucks	2006–07
5	Evgeni Nabokov	46	Sharks	2007–08
6	Miikka Kiprusoff	45	Flames	2008–09
	Martin Brodeur	45	Devils	2009–10
8	Eight players tied with 44			

▲ Roberto Luongo

▲ Braden Holtby

RECORD FACT

Longevity as a goaltender means a lot of wins. It can also mean a lot of losses. Martin Brodeur, the all-time wins leader, also holds the record for career losses, with 397. Roberto Luongo is second, with 376. Gary Smith of the Golden Seals holds the record for most losses in a single season, with 48 in 1970–71.

Goalie Wins

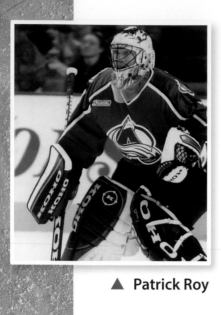

▲ Patrick Roy

CAREER

1	Martin Brodeur	691	Devils/Blues	1991–2015
2	Patrick Roy	551	Canadiens/Avalanche	1984–2003
3	Ed Belfour	484	Blackhawks/Sharks/Stars/Maple Leafs/Panthers	1988–2007
4	Roberto Luongo	471	Islanders/Canucks/Panthers	1999–2018*
5	Curtis Joseph	454	Blues/Oilers/Maple Leafs/Red Wings/Coyotes/Flames	1989–2009
6	Terry Sawchuk	445	Red Wings/Bruins/Maple Leafs/Kings/Rangers	1949–1970
7	Jacques Plante	437	Canadiens/Rangers/Blues/Maple Leafs/Bruins	1952–1973
8	Henrik Lundqvist	431	Rangers	2005–2018*
9	Tony Esposito	423	Canadiens/Blackhawks	1968–1984
10	Glenn Hall	407	Red Wings/Blackhawks/Blues	1952–1971

KEEP ON WINNING

Gilles Gilbert of the Bruins holds the record for consecutive victories. He won 17 games in a row in 1975–76. Another Bruins netminder, Gerry Cheevers, has the record for the longest undefeated streak. He went 32 games without a loss in 1971–72, with 24 wins and eight ties. (The NHL had ties before introducing the shootout in 2005.)

▲ Gerry Cheevers

Goals-Against Average

SINGLE SEASON

1	**George Hainsworth**	0.92	Canadiens	1928–29
2	**George Hainsworth**	1.06	Canadiens	1927–28
3	**Alec Connell**	1.12	Senators	1925–26
4	**Tiny Thompson**	1.15	Bruins	1928–29
5	**Roy Worters**	1.16	Americans	1928–29
6	**Alec Connell**	1.24	Senators	1927–28
7	**Dolly Dolson**	1.38	Cougars	1928–29
8	**John Ross Roach**	1.41	Rangers	1928–29
9	**Clint Benedict**	1.42	Maroons	1926–27
10	**Alec Connell**	1.43	Senators	1928–29

▲ Dominik Hašek

CAREER

1	**Alec Connell**	1.92	Senators/Falcons/Americans/Maroons	1924–1937
2	**George Hainsworth**	1.93	Canadiens/Maple Leafs	1926–1937
3	**Charlie Gardiner**	2.02	Blackhawks	1927–1934
4	**Lorne Chabot**	2.03	Rangers/Maple Leafs/Canadiens/Blackhawks/Maroons/Americans	1926–1937
5	**Tiny Thompson**	2.07	Bruins/Red Wings	1928–1940
6	**Dave Kerr**	2.14	Maroons/Americans/Rangers	1930–1941
7	**Dominik Hašek**	2.2	Blackhawks/Sabres/Red Wings/Senators	1990–2008
8	**Ken Dryden**	2.24	Canadiens	1970–1979
9	**Martin Brodeur**	2.24	Devils/Blues	1991–2015
10	**Tuukka Rask**	2.26	Bruins	2007–2018*

active player

RECORD FACT

Goals-against average (GAA) is a stat that shows how many goals per game are allowed by the goalie. To calculate the GAA, take the number of goals allowed and multiply by 60 (for a 60-minute game). Then divide the result by the number of minutes played.

Goals Allowed

SINGLE SEASON

1	**Ken McAuley**	310	Rangers	1943–44
2	**Greg Millen**	282	Whalers	1982–83
3	**Greg Millen**	258	Penguins	1980–81
4	**Gary Smith**	256	Golden Seals	1970–71
5	**Craig Billington**	254	Senators	1993–94
6	**Mike Liut**	250	Blues	1981–82
	Peter Sidorkiewicz	250	Senators	1992–93
8	**Tony Esposito**	246	Blackhawks	1980–81
	Grant Fuhr	246	Oilers	1987–88
10	**Harry Lumley**	245	Blackhawks	1950–51

▲ Mike Liut

CAREER

1	**Martin Brodeur**	2,781	Devils/Blues	1991–2015
2	**Grant Fuhr**	2,756	Oilers/Maple Leafs/Sabres/Kings/Blues/Flames	1981–2000
3	**Gilles Meloche**	2,755	Blackhawks/Golden Seals/Barons/North Stars/Penguins	1970–1988
4	**Tony Esposito**	2,563	Canadiens/Blackhawks	1968–1984
5	**Patrick Roy**	2,546	Canadiens/Avalanche	1984–2003
6	**Curtis Joseph**	2,516	Blues/Oilers/Maple Leafs/Red Wings/Coyotes/Flames	1989–2009
7	**John Vanbiesbrouck**	2,502	Rangers/Panthers/Flyers/Islanders/Devils	1981–2002
8	**Gump Worsley**	2,398	Rangers/Canadiens/North Stars	1952–1974
9	**Roberto Luongo**	2,393	Islanders/Canucks/Panthers	1999–2018*
10	**Terry Sawchuk**	2,385	Red Wings/Bruins/Maple Leafs/Kings/Rangers	1949–1970
	Tom Barrasso	2,385	Sabres/Penguins/Senators/Hurricanes/Maple Leafs/Blues	1983–2003

RECORD FACT

Terry Sawchuk ended up with more ties on his record than any other goalie. He finished in a stalemate 171 times in 21 seasons. That record will never be broken because the NHL now breaks regular-season ties with a shootout.

Save Percentage

SINGLE SEASON

1	**Jacques Plante**	0.9437	Maple Leafs	1970–71
2	**Craig Anderson**	0.9409	Senators	2012–13
3	**Jacques Plante**	0.9404	Blues	1968–69
4	**Brian Elliott**	0.9403	Blues	2011–12
5	**Tim Thomas**	0.9382	Bruins	2010–11
6	**Dominik Hašek**	0.9366	Sabres	1998–99
7	**Cory Schneider**	0.9365	Canucks	2011–12
8	**Bruce Gamble**	0.9343	Maple Leafs	1967–68
9	**Johnny Bower**	0.9341	Maple Leafs	1967–68
10	**Tony Esposito**	0.9339	Blackhawks	1971–72

▲ Craig Anderson

CAREER

1	**Dominik Hašek**	0.9223	Blackhawks/Sabres/ Red Wings/Senators	1990–2008
2	**Tuukka Rask**	0.9221	Bruins	2007–2018*
3	**Johnny Bower**	0.9219	Rangers/Maple Leafs	1953–1970
4	**Ken Dryden**	0.9215	Canadiens	1970–1979
5	**Cory Schneider**	0.9201	Canucks/Devils	2008–2018*
6	**Sergei Bobrovsky**	0.92	Flyers/Blue Jackets	2010–2018*
7	**Tim Thomas**	0.9199	Bruins/Panthers/Stars	2002–2014
8	**Jacques Plante**	0.9196	Canadiens/Rangers/Blues/ Maple Leafs/Bruins	1952–1973
9	**Roberto Luongo**	0.9195	Islanders/Canucks/Panthers	1999–2018*
10	**Braden Holtby**	0.9194	Capitals	2010–2018*

active player

RECORD FACT

Save percentage is a stat that shows how often a goalie stops the other team from scoring. To calculate the save percentage, divide the number of saves a goalie makes by the total number of shots on goal. A goalie who made 270 saves on 300 shots on goal would have a save percentage of 0.900.

Saves

▲ Cam Ward

SINGLE SEASON

1	**Gump Worsley**	2,376	Rangers	1955–56
2	**Gump Worsley**	2,306	Rangers	1962–63
3	**Roberto Luongo**	2,303	Panthers	2003–04
4	**Roberto Luongo**	2,275	Panthers	2005–06
5	**Eddie Johnston**	2,243	Bruins	1963–64
6	**Jacques Plante**	2,224	Rangers	1963–64
7	**Felix Potvin**	2,214	Maple Leafs	1996–97
8	**Cam Ward**	2,191	Hurricanes	2010–11
9	**Marc Denis**	2,172	Blue Jackets	2002–03
10	**Curtis Joseph**	2,169	Blues	1993–94

CAREER

1	**Martin Brodeur**	28,928	Devils/Blues	1991–2015
2	**Roberto Luongo**	27,326	Islanders/Canucks/Panthers	1999–2018*
3	**Patrick Roy**	25,800	Canadiens/Avalanche	1984–2003
4	**Tony Esposito**	24,761	Canadiens/Blackhawks	1968–1984
5	**Glenn Hall**	24,610	Red Wings/Blackhawks/Blues	1952–1971
6	**Curtis Joseph**	24,279	Blues/Oilers/Maple Leafs/Red Wings/Coyotes/Flames	1989–2009
7	**Ed Belfour**	22,433	Blackhawks/Sharks/Stars/Maple Leafs/Panthers	1988–2007
8	**John Vanbiesbrouck**	22,203	Rangers/Panthers/Flyers/Islanders/Devils	1981–2002
9	**Gump Worsley**	21,766	Rangers/Canadiens/North Stars	1952–1974
10	**Grant Fuhr**	21,615	Oilers/Maple Leafs/Sabres/Kings/Blues/Flames	1981–2000

active player

Shutouts

▲ George Hainsworth

SINGLE SEASON

1	**George Hainsworth**	22	Canadiens	1928–29
2	**Alec Connell**	15	Senators	1925–26
	Alec Connell	15	Senators	1927–28
	Hal Winkler	15	Bruins	1927–28
	Tony Esposito	15	Blackhawks	1969–70
6	**George Hainsworth**	14	Canadiens	1926–27
7	**Seven players tied with 13**			

▲ Tony Esposito

Shutouts

CAREER

1	**Martin Brodeur**	125	Devils/Blues	1991–2015
2	**Terry Sawchuk**	103	Red Wings/Bruins/Maple Leafs/Kings/Rangers	1949–1970
3	**George Hainsworth**	94	Canadiens/Maple Leafs	1926–1937
4	**Glenn Hall**	84	Red Wings/Blackhawks/Blues	1952–1971
5	**Jacques Plante**	82	Canadiens/Rangers/Blues/Maple Leafs/Bruins	1952–1973
6	**Alec Connell**	81	Senators/Falcons/Americans/Maroons	1924–1937
	Tiny Thompson	81	Bruins/Red Wings	1928–1940
	Dominik Hašek	81	Blackhawks/Sabres/Red Wings/Senators	1990–2008
9	**Tony Esposito**	76	Canadiens/Blackhawks	1968–1984
	Ed Belfour	76	Blackhawks/Sharks/Stars/Maple Leafs/Panthers	1988–2007
	Roberto Luongo	76	Islanders/Canucks/Panthers	1999–2018*

Games Played

CAREER

1	**Martin Brodeur**	1,266	Devils/Blues	1991–2015
2	**Patrick Roy**	1,029	Canadiens/Avalanche	1984–2003
3	**Roberto Luongo**	1,001	Islanders/Canucks/Panthers	1999–2018*
4	**Terry Sawchuk**	971	Red Wings/Bruins/Maple Leafs/Kings/Rangers	1949–1970
5	**Ed Belfour**	963	Blackhawks/Sharks/Stars/Maple Leafs/Panthers	1988–2007
6	**Curtis Joseph**	943	Blues/Oilers/Maple Leafs/Red Wings/Coyotes/Flames	1989–2009
7	**Glenn Hall**	906	Red Wings/Blackhawks/Blues	1952–1971
8	**Tony Esposito**	886	Canadiens/Blackhawks	1968–1984
9	**John Vanbiesbrouck**	882	Rangers/Panthers/Flyers/Islanders/Devils	1981–2002
10	**Grant Fuhr**	868	Oilers/Maple Leafs/Sabres/Kings/Blues/Flames	1981–2000

active player

Goals For Goalies

Goaltenders don't get the glory of the great goal scorers. However, goalies have proven they can score, once in a while. Fourteen times in NHL history, goaltenders have been credited for scoring goals. For some, they were simply the last offensive player to touch the puck before a defensive player put the puck in his own net. However, some have shot and scored into an open net. Martin Brodeur is the only goalie to be credited for three goals. Ron Hextall was the first goalie to shoot and score—and he did it twice.

▲ **Ron Hextall**

GOALS BY GOALIES

Billy Smith	Islanders	Nov. 28, 1979
Ron Hextall	Flyers	Dec. 8, 1987*
Ron Hextall	Flyers	Apr. 11, 1989*
Chris Osgood	Red Wings	Mar. 6, 1996*
Martin Brodeur	Devils	Apr. 17, 1997*
Damian Rhodes	Senators	Jan. 2, 1999
Martin Brodeur	Devils	Feb. 15, 2000
Jose Theodore	Canadiens	Jan. 2, 2001*
Evgeni Nabokov	Sharks	Mar. 10, 2002*
Mika Noronen	Sabres	Feb. 14, 2004
Chris Mason	Predators	Apr. 15, 2006
Cam Ward	Hurricanes	Dec. 26, 2011
Martin Brodeur	Devils	Mar. 21, 2013
Mike Smith	Coyotes	Oct. 19, 2013*

shot on goal

RECORD FACT

In 1993, Flames goaltender Jeff Reese assisted on three goals in a 13-1 victory over the Sharks. That set a record for points in a game by a goaltender.

Team Records

On February 1, 2018, the Vegas Golden Knights won their 34th regular-season game. That set a record for the most wins by an NHL team in its first year of existence. It was an impressive record, passing the previous number of 33 set by the Ducks and Panthers in 1993–94.

But that was just the beginning.

Vegas shocked the world by winning 51 games that season. He cruised all the way to the Stanley Cup Finals before the team fell to the Washington Capitals. The Golden Knights proved that hockey is indeed one of the greatest team games in sports. Goal scorers, passers, defenders, and goaltenders work in concert to win games. Those that win a lot capture championships—and set records.

Records set by the Golden Knights that first season won't be forgotten. They'll go down in history along with superb standards set by the Montreal Canadiens, Edmonton Oilers, and Detroit Red Wings.

Most Wins

SINGLE SEASON

1	Red Wings	62	1995–96
2	Canadiens	60	1976–77
3	Canadiens	59	1977–78
4	Canadiens	58	1975–76
	Red Wings	58	2005–06
6	Bruins	57	1970–71
	Oilers	57	1983–84
8	Oilers	56	1985–86
	Penguins	56	1992–93
	Capitals	56	2015–16

Fewest Wins

SINGLE SEASON

1	Capitals	8	1974–75
2	Jets	9	1980–81
	Senators	9	1994–95
4	Senators	10	1992–93
5	Capitals	11	1975–76
	Sharks	11	1992–93
7	Blackhawks	12	1953–54
	Islanders	12	1972–73
	Scouts	12	1975–76
	Nordiques	12	1989–90

RECORD FACT

The most- and fewest-wins records come from the era in which the NHL played 70 games or more. The NHL schedule expanded from 60 to 70 games starting in the 1949–50 season. Today, the NHL plays an 82-game schedule.

Streaks

SINGLE SEASON

Winning Streak	The Penguins won 17 games in a row during the 1992–93 season.
Unbeaten Streak	The Flyers did not lose a game in 35-straight contests during the 1979–80 season, going 25–0–10.
Losing Streak	The 1974–75 Capitals and 1992–93 Sharks share the record for losing 17 games in a row.
Winless Streak	The Jets went 0–23–7, a streak of 30 games in a row without a win, in the 1980–81 season.

▲ Flames, 1988

Goals Scored

SINGLE SEASON

1	**Oilers**	446	1983–84
2	**Oilers**	426	1985–86
3	**Oilers**	424	1982–83
4	**Oilers**	417	1981–82
5	**Oilers**	401	1984–85
6	**Bruins**	399	1970–71
7	**Flames**	397	1987–88
8	**Canadiens**	387	1976–77
9	**Islanders**	385	1981–82
10	**Kings**	376	1988–89

Goals Allowed

SINGLE SEASON

1	Capitals	446	1974–75
2	Red Wings	415	1985–86
3	Sharks	414	1992–93
4	Nordiques	407	1989–90
5	Whalers	403	1982–83
6	Canucks	401	1984–85
7	Jets	400	1980–81
8	Senators	397	1993–94
9	Senators	395	1992–93
10	Capitals	394	1975–76
	Penguins	394	1982–83

Most Goals in a Game

COMBINED GOALS

1	Canadiens	14	St. Patricks	7	21	Jan. 10, 1920
	Oilers	12	Blackhawks	9	21	Dec. 11, 1985
3	Oilers	12	North Stars	8	20	Jan. 4, 1984
	Maple Leafs	11	Oilers	9	20	Jan. 8, 1986
5	Wanderers	10	Arenas	9	19	Dec. 19, 1917
	Canadiens	16	Bulldogs	3	19	Mar. 3, 1920
	Canadiens	13	Tigers	6	19	Feb. 26, 1921
	Bruins	10	Rangers	9	19	Mar. 4, 1944
	Red Wings	10	Bruins	9	19	Mar. 16, 1944
	Canucks	10	North Stars	9	19	Oct. 7, 1983

SINGLE-PERIOD SCORING

The Sabres scored nine goals in a single period of play on March 19, 1981, en route to a 14-4 victory over the Maple Leafs. The Leafs also scored three times in that period. Those 12 combined goals are tied for the NHL record. The Oilers and Blackhawks each scored six goals during a period on December 11, 1985. The Oilers went on to win 12-9.

CHAPTER 4

Stanley Cup Playoffs

With back-to-back Stanley Cups in 2016 and 2017, the Pittsburgh Penguins moved into an exclusive club. The two championships, led by Sidney Crosby, gave the Penguins five titles. This is something only six other franchises have achieved. Still, it's a long way from the record of 24 championships held by the Montreal Canadiens.

Every NHL team starts the season aiming to make the playoffs. The ultimate prize is making it to the Stanley Cup Finals and winning a championship.

The postseason has featured many outstanding, memorable performances. Some of those performances have put players and teams into the record books. When a record leads to a championship, it's that much sweeter.

Crosby has climbed up the ladder of playoff points, entering the top 10 in 2018. His old teammate, Marc-André Fleury, has proven to be one of the all-time great playoff goalies, putting up big numbers for the Penguins as well as for the Golden Knights.

● PLAYOFF RECORDS

MOST CHAMPIONSHIPS

1	Canadiens	24
2	Maple Leafs	13
3	Red Wings	11
4	Blackhawks	6
	Bruins	6
6	Oilers	5
	Penguins	5
8	Islanders	4
	Rangers	4
10	Devils	3

Dynasties

The **Montreal Canadiens** are the only team to win five consecutive championships. They won the Stanley Cup each year from 1956 through 1960. The Canadiens also won four in a row from 1976 through 1979. The only other team to win four in a row is the **New York Islanders**, who were champions from 1980 through 1983. The Islanders won a record 19 playoff series in a row over that time before losing to the Oilers in the 1984 Stanley Cup Finals.

▲ 1960 Montreal Canadiens

RECORD FACT

The Canadiens have appeared in the Stanley Cup Finals a record 34 times. The Red Wings are next at 24, followed by the Maple Leafs at 21. However, the Leafs have not made it to a final since 1967.

Playoff Appearances

TEAM

#	Team	
1	Canadiens	83
2	Bruins	71
3	Maple Leafs	67
4	Red Wings	64
5	Blackhawks	62
6	Rangers	59
7	Blues	41
8	Flyers	39
9	Penguins	33
10	Stars	31

Most Championships

PLAYER

#	Player		Team
1	Henri Richard	11	Canadiens
2	Jean Beliveau	10	Canadiens
3	Claude Provost	9	Canadiens
4	Yvan Cournoyer	8	Canadiens
	Red Kelly	8	Red Wings/Maple Leafs
	Jacques Lemaire	8	Canadiens
	Maurice Richard	8	Canadiens
8	Serge Savard	7	Canadiens
	Jean-Guy Talbot	7	Canadiens
9	15 players tied with 6		

Playoff Goals

SINGLE SEASON

1	**Reggie Leach**	19	Flyers	1976
	Jari Kurri	19	Oilers	1985
3	**Joe Sakic**	18	Avalanche	1996
4	**Mike Bossy**	17	Islanders	1981
	Steve Payne	17	North Stars	1981
	Mike Bossy	17	Islanders	1982
	Mike Bossy	17	Islanders	1983
	Wayne Gretzky	17	Oilers	1985
	Kevin Stevens	17	Penguins	1991
10	**Six players tied with 16**			

▲ Mike Bossy

CAREER

1	**Wayne Gretzky**	122	Oilers/Kings/Blues/Rangers	16 playoffs
2	**Mark Messier**	109	Oilers/Rangers	17 playoffs
3	**Jari Kurri**	106	Oilers/Kings/Rangers/Ducks/Avalanche	15 playoffs
4	**Brett Hull**	103	Flames/Blues/Stars/Red Wings	19 playoffs
5	**Glenn Anderson**	93	Oilers/Maple Leafs/Rangers/Blues	15 playoffs
6	**Mike Bossy**	85	Islanders	10 playoffs
7	**Joe Sakic**	84	Nordiques/Avalanche	13 playoffs
8	**Maurice Richard**	82	Canadiens	15 playoffs
9	**Claude Lemieux**	80	Canadiens/Devils/Avalanche/Coyotes/Stars/Sharks	18 playoffs
10	**Jean Beliveau**	79	Canadiens	17 playoffs

▲ Mark Messier

Playoff Power-Play Goals

SINGLE SEASON

1	Mike Bossy	9	Islanders	1981
	Cam Neely	9	Bruins	1991
3	Tim Kerr	8	Flyers	1989
	John Druce	8	Capitals	1990
	Brian Propp	8	North Stars	1991
	Mario Lemieux	8	Penguins	1992
7	Eight players tied with 7			

▲ Brian Propp

Playoff Game Winners

SINGLE SEASON

1	Brad Richards	7	Lightning	2004
2	Joe Sakic	6	Avalanche	1996
	Joe Nieuwendyk	6	Stars	1999
4	Mike Bossy	5	Islanders	1983
	Jari Kurri	5	Oilers	1987
	Bobby Smith	5	North Stars	1991
	Mario Lemieux	5	Penguins	1992
	Fernando Pisani	5	Oilers	2006
	Johan Franzen	5	Red Wings	2008
	Dustin Byfuglien	5	Blackhawks	2010
	Jake Guentzel	5	Penguins	2017

RECORD FACT

Wayne Gretzky and Brett Hull have scored more game-winning playoff goals than any other players. Each netted 24 winners in his career. Joe Sakic has the record for overtime game-winners, scoring eight in his playoff career.

High Five

Five players have scored five goals in a single playoff game.

PLAYER		
Newsy Lalonde	Canadiens	1919
Maurice Richard	Canadiens	1944
Reggie Leach	Flyers	1976
Darryl Sittler	Maple Leafs	1976
Mario Lemieux	Penguins	1989

Overtime Winners

Sixteen players in NHL history have scored a goal in overtime that gave their team the Stanley Cup. In 2014, **Alec Martinez**'s double-overtime goal in Game 5 clinched the cup for the Kings against the Rangers. Two players, the Stars' **Brett Hull** in 1999 and the Avalanche's **Uwe Krupp** in 1996, won the cup with a goal in triple overtime. Two Red Wings players scored overtime goals in a Game 7, **Pete Babando** in double-OT in 1950 and **Tony Leswick** in 1954.

▲ Maurice Richard

▲ Mario Lemieux

RECORD FACT

Six players have scored three short-handed goals during a playoff run. Naturally, Wayne Gretzky was one of them, accomplishing the feat in 1983. Bill Barber, Lorne Henning, Todd Marchant, Wayne Presley, and Derek Sanderson complete the list. Mark Messier has the career record for short-handed playoff goals, scoring 14.

Playoff Assists

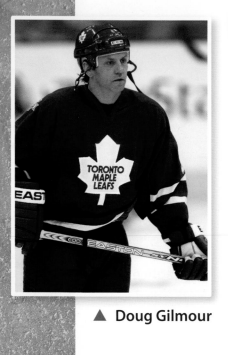

▲ Doug Gilmour

SINGLE SEASON

1	Wayne Gretzky	31	Oilers	1988
2	Wayne Gretzky	30	Oilers	1985
3	Wayne Gretzky	29	Oilers	1987
4	Mario Lemieux	28	Penguins	1991
5	Wayne Gretzky	26	Oilers	1983
6	Paul Coffey	25	Oilers	1985
	Doug Gilmour	25	Maple Leafs	1993
	Wayne Gretzky	25	Kings	1993
9	Al MacInnis	24	Flames	1989
	Mark Recchi	24	Penguins	1991

CAREER

1	Wayne Gretzky	260	Oilers/Kings/Blues/Rangers	16 playoffs
2	Mark Messier	186	Oilers/Rangers	17 playoffs
3	Ray Bourque	139	Bruins/Avalanche	21 playoffs
4	Paul Coffey	137	Oilers/Penguins/Kings/Red Wings/Flyers/Hurricanes	16 playoffs
5	Nicklas Lidstrom	129	Red Wings	20 playoffs
6	Doug Gilmour	128	Blues/Flames/Maple Leafs/Devils/Sabres/Canadiens	17 playoffs
7	Jari Kurri	127	Oilers/Kings/Rangers/Ducks/Avalanche	15 playoffs
8	Sergei Fedorov	124	Red Wings/Capitals	15 playoffs
9	Jaromír Jágr	123	Penguins/Capitals/Rangers/Flyers/Bruins/Panthers	18 playoffs
10	Glenn Anderson	121	Oilers/Maple Leafs/Rangers/Blues	15 playoffs
	Al MacInnis	121	Flames/Blues	19 playoffs

RECORD FACT

Wayne Gretzky of the Oilers and Mikko Leinonen of the Rangers each had a six-assist playoff game. Leinonen set the record in 1982, and Gretzky tied it in 1987.

Playoff Points

SINGLE SEASON

1	Wayne Gretzky	47	Oilers	1985
2	Mario Lemieux	44	Penguins	1991
3	Wayne Gretzky	43	Oilers	1988
4	Wayne Gretzky	40	Kings	1993
5	Wayne Gretzky	38	Oilers	1983
6	Paul Coffey	37	Oilers	1985
7	Evgeni Malkin	36	Penguins	2009
8	Mike Bossy	35	Islanders	1981
	Wayne Gretzky	35	Oilers	1984
	Doug Gilmour	35	Maple Leafs	1993

▲ Evgeni Malkin

CAREER

1	Wayne Gretzky	382	Oilers/Kings/Blues/Rangers	16 playoffs
2	Mark Messier	295	Oilers/Rangers	17 playoffs
3	Jari Kurri	233	Oilers/Kings/Rangers/Ducks/Avalanche	15 playoffs
4	Glenn Anderson	214	Oilers/Maple Leafs/Rangers/Blues	15 playoffs
5	Jaromír Jágr	201	Penguins/Capitals/Rangers/Flyers/Bruins/Panthers	18 playoffs
6	Paul Coffey	196	Oilers/Penguins/Kings/Red Wings/Whalers/Flyers/Blackhawks/Hurricanes/Bruins	16 playoffs
7	Brett Hull	190	Flames/Blues/Stars/Red Wings	19 playoffs
8	Doug Gilmour	188	Blues/Flames/Maple Leafs/Devils/Sabres/Canadiens	17 playoffs
	Joe Sakic	188	Nordiques/Avalance	13 playoffs
10	Sidney Crosby	185	Penguins	11 playoffs*
	Steve Yzerman	185	Red Wings	20 playoffs

active player

RECORD FACT

The record for points in a single playoff game is eight, set by two players. Patrik Sundstrom of the Devils did it first in 1988. The next year, the Penguins' Mario Lemieux matched the feat.

Playoff Games

▲ Nicklas
Lidstrom

	CAREER			
1	Chris Chelios	266	Canadiens/Blackhawks/Red Wings	24 playoffs
2	Nicklas Lidstrom	263	Red Wings	20 playoffs
3	Patrick Roy	247	Canadiens/Avalanche	17 playoffs
4	Mark Messier	236	Oilers/Rangers	17 playoffs
5	Claude Lemieux	234	Canadiens/Devils/Avalanche/Coyotes/Stars/Sharks	18 playoffs
6	Scott Stevens	233	Capitals/Blues/Devils	20 playoffs
7	Guy Carbonneau	231	Canadiens/Blues/Stars	17 playoffs
8	Larry Robinson	227	Canadiens/Kings	20 playoffs
9	Glenn Anderson	225	Oilers/Maple Leafs/Rangers/Blues	15 playoffs
10	Kris Draper	222	Jets/Red Wings	18 playoffs

Playoff Games by a Goalie

	CAREER			
1	Patrick Roy	247	Canadiens/Avalanche	17 playoffs
2	Martin Brodeur	205	Devils	17 playoffs
3	Ed Belfour	161	Blackhawks/Stars/Maple Leafs	13 playoffs
4	Grant Fuhr	150	Oilers/Sabres/Blues	14 playoffs
5	Mike Vernon	138	Flames/Red Wings/Sharks/Panthers	14 playoffs
6	Marc-André Fleury	135	Penguins/Golden Knights	12 playoffs*
7	Curtis Joseph	133	Blues/Oilers/Maple Leafs/Red Wings/Flames	14 playoffs
8	Andy Moog	132	Oilers/Bruins/Stars/Canadiens	16 playoffs
	Billy Smith	132	Kings/Islanders	13 playoffs
10	Chris Osgood	129	Red Wings/Islanders/Blues	13 playoffs

Goalie Playoff Wins

CAREER

1	**Patrick Roy**	151	Canadiens/Avalanche	17 playoffs
2	**Martin Brodeur**	113	Devils	17 playoffs
3	**Grant Fuhr**	92	Oilers/Sabres/Blues	14 playoffs
4	**Ed Belfour**	88	Blackhawks/Stars/Maple Leafs	13 playoffs
	Billy Smith	88	Kings/Islanders	13 playoffs
6	**Ken Dryden**	80	Canadiens	8 playoffs
7	**Mike Vernon**	77	Flames/Red Wings/Sharks/Panthers	14 playoffs
8	**Marc-André Fleury**	75	Penguins/Golden Knights	12 playoffs*
9	**Chris Osgood**	74	Red Wings/Islanders/Blues	13 playoffs
10	**Jacques Plante**	71	Canadiens/Blues/Maple Leafs/Bruins	16 playoffs

* active player

▲ **Ed Belfour**

THE STANLEY CUP

The oldest and most famous trophy in professional sports in North America is the Stanley Cup. It goes to the NHL champion each year. One of the things that makes the cup special is that each member of the winning team gets his name engraved on it. The name of Henri Richard of the Canadiens is etched into the silver trophy 11 times—more than any other player. However, Jean Beliveau of the Canadiens has his name on it more than any other person. It's on there 10 times as a player and another seven as a member of the team's management.

Playoff Goals-Against Average (minimum 25 games)

▲ Terry Sawchuk

▲ Turk Broda

SINGLE SEASON (MIN. 5 GAMES)

1	**Alec Connell**	0.60	Senators	1927
	Tiny Thompson	0.60	Bruins	1929
3	**Terry Sawchuk**	0.63	Red Wings	1952
4	**George Hainsworth**	0.75	Canadiens	1930
5	**John Ross Roach**	0.77	Rangers	1929
6	**Clint Benedict**	0.86	Maroons	1928
7	**Dave Kerr**	1.09	Rangers	1937
8	**Turk Broda**	1.10	Maple Leafs	1951
9	**Alec Connell**	1.12	Maroons	1935
10	**Tiny Thompson**	1.23	Bruins	1933

CAREER

1	**Clint Benedict**	1.22	Senators/Maroons	8 playoffs
2	**Lorne Chabot**	1.51	Rangers/Maple Leafs/Canadiens/Blackhawks/Maroons	9 playoffs
3	**John Ross Roach**	1.63	St. Patricks/Rangers/Red Wings	7 playoffs
4	**Dave Kerr**	1.74	Maroons/Rangers	9 playoffs
5	**Patrick Lalime**	1.77	Senators	4 playoffs
6	**Gerry McNeil**	1.84	Canadiens	5 playoffs
7	**Tiny Thompson**	1.88	Bruins/Red Wings	10 playoffs
8	**George Hainsworth**	1.93	Canadiens/Maple Leafs	10 playoffs
9	**Turk Broda**	1.98	Maple Leafs	13 playoffs
10	**Martin Brodeur**	2.02	Devils	17 playoffs

Playoff Save Percentage *(minimum 25 games)*

SINGLE SEASON *(MIN. 5 GAMES)*

1	**Bernie Parent**	0.963	Flyers	1968
2	**Rogie Vachon**	0.953	Canadiens	1969
3	**Marty Turco**	0.952	Stars	2007
4	**Jacques Plante**	0.950	Canadiens	1960
	Jacques Plante	0.950	Blues	1969
	Dominik Hašek	0.950	Sabres	1994
7	**Johnny Bower**	0.949	Maple Leafs	1963
8	**Gerry Cheevers**	0.947	Bruins	1969
	Frederik Andersen	0.947	Ducks	2016
10	**Jonathan Quick**	0.946	Kings	2012

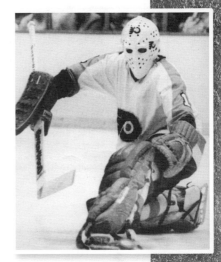

▲ Bernie Parent

CAREER

1	**Tim Thomas**	0.933	Bruins/Stars	5 playoffs
2	**Jonas Hiller**	0.930	Ducks/Flames	4 playoffs
3	**Craig Anderson**	0.929	Avalanche/Senators	5 playoffs*
	Braden Holtby	0.929	Capitals	6 playoffs*
5	**Ben Bishop**	0.927	Lightning	2 playoffs*
	Olaf Kolzig	0.927	Capitals	6 playoffs
7	**Martin Jones**	0.926	Kings/Sharks	4 playoffs*
	Patrick Lalime	0.926	Senators	4 playoffs
9	**Jean-Sébastien Giguère**	0.925	Ducks	5 playoffs
	Dominik Hašek	0.925	Blackhawks/Sabres/Red Wings	13 playoffs

* active player

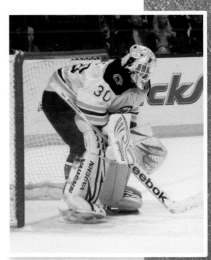

▲ Tim Thomas

Playoff Shutouts

▲ Nikolai Khabibulin

SINGLE SEASON				
1	**Martin Brodeur**	7	Devils	2003
2	**Dominik Hašek**	6	Red Wings	2002
3	**Nikolai Khabibulin**	5	Lightning	2004
	Miikka Kiprusoff	5	Flames	2004
	Jean-Sébastien Giguère	5	Ducks	2003
6	**16 players tied with 4**			

HIGH STAKES

The Kings defeated the Oilers 10-8 in postseason game on April 7, 1982. The 18 goals were the most scored by two teams in a Stanley Cup playoff game. In 1989, the Penguins and Flyers came close to matching that, scoring 17 in a 10-7 Pittsburgh victory. The most goals scored by one team in a playoff game is 13, racked up by the Oilers in a 13-3 win over the Kings on April 9, 1987.

▲ Wayne Gretzky

Playoff Shutouts

CAREER

1	**Martin Brodeur**	24	Devils	17 playoffs
2	**Patrick Roy**	23	Canadiens/Avalanche	17 playoffs
3	**Curtis Joseph**	16	Blues/Oilers/Maple Leafs/Red Wings/Flames	14 playoffs
4	**Chris Osgood**	15	Red Wings/Islanders/Blues	13 playoffs
5	**Ed Belfour**	14	Blackhawks/Stars/Maple Leafs	13 playoffs
	Marc-André Fleury	14	Penguins/Golden Knights	12 playoffs*
	Dominik Hašek	14	Blackhawks/Sabres/Red Wings	13 playoffs
	Jacques Plante	14	Canadiens/Blues/Maple Leafs/Bruins	16 playoffs
9	**Turk Broda**	13	Maple Leafs	13 playoffs
10	**Terry Sawchuk**	12	Red Wings/Maple Leafs/Kings/Rangers	15 playoffs

active player

▲ **Curtis Joseph**

▼ **Ed Belfour**

PLAYING TILL THE END

One of the most exciting things about playoff hockey is that games are played until a winning goal is scored. There are no ties or shootouts. For the game's two goalies, all of the pressure is on them. Ed Belfour was great under pressure, winning 22 overtime games in the playoffs, including a triple-OT win in Game 6 of the 1999 finals that clinched the Stanley Cup for the Stars. A year later, though, he gave up the cup-winning goal to the Devils' Jason Arnott.

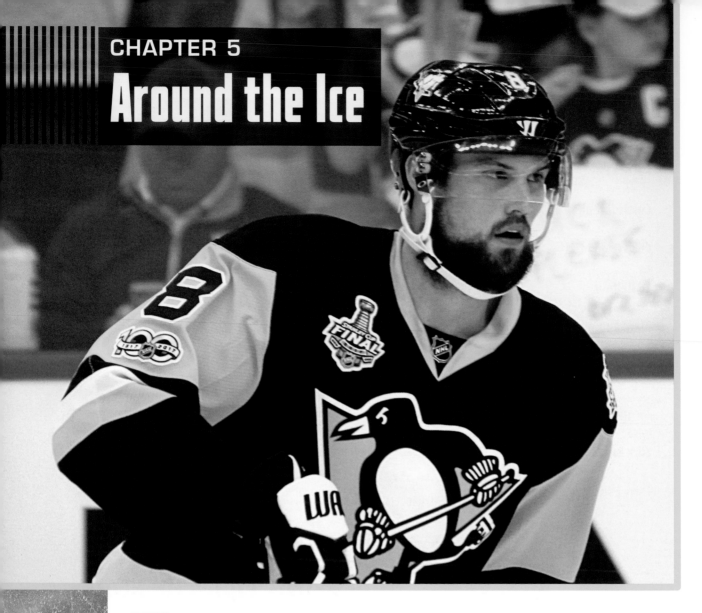

CHAPTER 5

Around the Ice

There's an old saying that records are made to be broken. That might be true, but some records appear to be so far out of reach that it would take an extraordinary effort to beat them.

During the 2018 Stanley Cup playoffs, the Pittsburgh Penguins' Evgeni Malkin and Brian Dumoulin scored goals five seconds apart. That tied a record that had been set 53 years earlier. That still wasn't as fast as the regular-season record of three seconds, a feat that has been accomplished three times. Could one team ever get the record to two seconds?

Will anyone challenge Wayne Gretzky's 51-game point-scoring streak, or get near Scotty Bowman's 1,244 victories as a coach? Will we ever see a playoff game go into a seventh overtime, knocking out the two that went six extra periods?

Which of the following records do you think might be broken someday?

FASTEST GOAL TO START A GAME

1	**Merlyn Phillips**	5 seconds	Maroons	1926
	Doug Smail	5 seconds	Jets	1981
	Bryan Trottier	5 seconds	Islanders	1984
	Alexander Mogilny	5 seconds	Sabres	1991
5	**Henry Boucha**	6 seconds	Red Wings	1973
	Jean Pronovost	6 seconds	Penguins	1976
	Alex Burrows	6 seconds	Canucks	2013
8	**Charlie Conacher**	7 seconds	Maple Leafs	1932
	Danny Gare	7 seconds	Sabres	1978
	Tiger Williams	7 seconds	Kings	1987
	Evgeni Malkin	7 seconds	Penguins	2011

▲ Alexander Mogilny

LONGEST GAMES

1	Red Wings, 1	Maroons, 0	2:56:30 (6 OT)	Mar. 24, 1936
2	Maple Leafs, 1	Bruins, 0	2:44:46 (6 OT)	Apr. 3, 1933
3	Flyers, 2	Penguins, 1	2:32:01 (5 OT)	May 4, 2000
4	Ducks, 4	Stars, 3	2:20:48 (5 OT)	Apr. 24, 2003
5	Penguins, 3	Capitals, 2	2:19:15 (4 OT)	Apr. 24, 1996
6	Canucks, 5	Stars, 4	2:18:06 (4 OT)	Apr. 11, 2007
7	Maple Leafs, 3	Red Wings, 2	2:10:18 (4 OT)	Mar. 23, 1943
8	Stars, 2	Sharks, 1	2:09:03 (4 OT)	May 4, 2008
9	Canadiens, 2	Rangers, 1	2:08:52 (4 OT)	Mar. 28, 1930
10	Islander, 3	Capitals, 2	2:08:47 (4 OT)	Apr. 18, 1987

RECORD FACT

The shortest overtime game in playoff history lasted just nine seconds. The Canadiens' Brian Skrudland ended it with a goal to defeat the Flames on May 18, 1986.

FAST, FASTER, FASTEST

The fastest goal to start a period is four seconds. The Maple Leafs' **James van Riemsdyk** did that in 2014, matching feats by the Blackhawks' **Denis Savard** in 1986 and the Canadiens' **Claude Provost** in 1957.

The fastest one team has scored two goals is three seconds. In 2016, the Islanders' **Anders Lee** and **Nikolay Kulemin** became the third pair to do it. The Wild did it during a game in 2004, and the St. Louis Eagles did it in 1935. The fastest one player has scored two goals is four seconds. It was done twice, by the Maroons' **Nels Stewart** in 1931 and the Jets' **Deron Quint** in 1995.

The fastest a team has scored two goals in a playoff game is five seconds. The Penguins did that in 2018, getting goals from **Evgeni Malkin** and **Brian Dumoulin**. That tied a record held since 1965 by the Red Wings.

In a span of two seconds, the Wild and the Blue Jackets each scored a goal against each other, the fastest two goals ever in a game. The Blues and Bruins also scored two seconds apart in 1987. In 1983, it took the North Stars and Rangers 15 seconds to score three goals.

Bill Mosienko of the Blackhawks scored the fastest hat trick in NHL history. In 1952, it took him just 21 seconds to score three goals.

▲ Evgeni Malkin

▲ James van Riemsdyk

SCORING STREAK

Wayne Gretzky started the 1983–84 season with a record 51-game point-scoring streak. The "Great One" racked up 153 points during the streak. The closest anyone has come to matching such a stretch is **Mario Lemieux**, who scored points in 46 straight games in 1989–90. The longest goal-scoring streak is 16 games, set by **Punch Broadbent** of the Senators in 1921–22.

▲ Wayne Gretzky

▲ Jacques Plante

AWARD WINNERS

Wayne Gretzky won the Hart Memorial Trophy as the NHL's most valuable player a record nine times. The next-highest on the list is **Gordie Howe**, who won it six times. **Bobby Orr** won the James Norris Memorial Trophy as the league's top defenseman eight times. Goaltending great **Jacques Plante** won the Vezina Trophy as the best goalie seven times.

CONSECUTIVE GAMES

When you think of "Ironman" streaks, baseball's Cal Ripken Jr. and football's Brett Favre come to mind. But the NHL has an Ironman, too. **Doug Jarvis** played in 964 consecutive games for the Canadiens, Capitals, and Whalers between 1975 and 1987.

Perhaps the most impressive Ironman streak belongs to **Glenn Hall**, a goaltender who played in 502 straight games—551 if you count playoff games. For seven years with the Red Wings and Blackhawks, Hall never missed a start. And he played at a time when most goalies didn't wear face protection. Today most goalies don't complete a season without taking games off to rest.

The Bruins defeated the Blackhawks on March 4, 1941. But if it weren't for Chicago goalie **Sam LoPresti**, the game would have been a blowout. The Bruins put a record 83 shots on goal that day, and LoPresti set a record of his own by stopping 80 of them.

Many of the NHL's shutout records were set when attacking teams were not allowed to pass the puck forward in the offensive zone. The longest shutout streak by a goaltender lasted 461 minutes, 29 seconds. **Alec Connell** of the Senators set that record in 1928, a stretch that included six-straight shutouts along the way. In the modern era, the Coyotes' **Brian Boucher** had five consecutive shutouts in 2003–04. He held opponents scoreless for 332 minutes, 1 second.

▲ Glenn Hall

▲ Brian Boucher

Most Shootout Goals

1	Frans Nielsen	48	Islanders/Red Wings*	2002–2016
2	Radim Vrbata	45	Avalanche/Hurricanes/ Blackhawks/Coyotes/Lightning/ Canucks/Panthers*	1997–2009
3	Zach Parise	42	Devils/Wild*	2004–2018*
	Jonathan Toews	42	Blackhawks*	1997–2013
5	Mikko Koivu	41	Wild*	1999–2012

Most Shootout Wins by a Goalie

SINGLE SEASON

1	Ryan Miller	59	Sabres/Blues/Canucks/Ducks*	2017*
2	Henrik Lundqvist	58	Rangers*	2010*
3	Marc-André Fleury	54	Penguins/Golden Knights*	2011*
4	Roberto Luongo	52	Islanders/Canucks/Panthers*	2013*
5	Martin Brodeur	42	Devils/Blues	2006
	Kari Lehtonen	42	Thrashers/Stars*	2001
	Jonathan Quick	42	Kings*	2017

active player

RECORD FACT

One of the most exciting shootout goals in hockey history took place in the 2018 Winter Olympics in South Korea. Jocelyne Lamoureux-Davidson made an incredible move to fake out the goalie and score, helping lift the United States women's hockey team to a win over Canada in the gold-medal game.

THE SHOOTOUT

Starting in 2005, the NHL adopted the shootout to break ties if neither team scores in overtime of a regular-season game. Each team selects three players who alternate shooting penalty shots—one-on-one plays against the goalie. The team with the most goals at the end of the shootout wins the game. Ilya Kovalchuk of the Devils has the record for most successful shootouts in a single season, scoring 11 times during 2011–12. In 2015, the NHL made overtimes a 3-on-3 game to try to break the tie before getting to a shootout.

Coaching Wins

REGULAR SEASON

1	**Scotty Bowman**	1,244	Blues/Canadiens/Sabres/Penguins/Red Wings	1967–2002
2	**Joel Quenneville**	884	Blues/Avalanche/Blackhawks	1996–2018*
3	**Ken Hitchcock**	823	Stars/Flyers/Blue Jackets/Blues	1995–2018
4	**Al Arbour**	782	Blues/Islanders	1970–2008
5	**Barry Trotz**	762	Predators/Capitals	1998–2018*

PLAYOFFS

1	**Scotty Bowman**	223	Blues/Canadiens/Sabres/Penguins/Red Wings	1967–2002
2	**Al Arbour**	123	Blues/Islanders	1970–2008
3	**Joel Quenneville**	118	Blues/Avalanche/Blackhawks	1996–2018*
4	**Dick Irvin**	100	Blackhawks/Maple Leafs/Canadiens	1928–1956
5	**Mike Keenan**	96	Flyers/Blackhawks/Rangers/Blues/Canucks/Bruins/Panthers/Flames	1984–2009

▲ Scotty Bowman

CHAMPIONSHIPS WON

1	**Scotty Bowman**	9	Canadiens/Penguins/Red Wings
2	**Toe Blake**	8	Canadiens
3	**Hap Day**	5	Maple Leafs
4	**Al Arbour**	4	Islanders
	Punch Imlach	4	Maple Leafs
	Dick Irvin	4	Maple Leafs/Canadiens
	Glen Sather	4	Oilers

active coach

INTERNATIONAL GAME

The NHL is a melting pot of the best hockey players from all over the world. Although many of the top record-breakers hail from Canada, there are exceptions. Jaromír Jágr is from the Czech Republic. Jari Kurri is from Finland. Chris Chelios is from the United States. Here are some of the top scorers from different nations:

Canada	**Wayne Gretzky**	2,857 points
Czech Republic	**Jaromír Jágr**	1,921 points
Finland	**Teemu Selänne**	1,451 points
United States	**Mike Modano**	1,374 points
Sweden	**Mats Sundin**	1,349 points
Russia	**Sergei Fedorov**	1,179 points
Slovenia	**Anže Kopitar**	828 points
Austria	**Thomas Vanek**	753 points

WOMEN'S HOCKEY

The popularity of women's hockey at the collegiate, international, and Olympic levels has led to professional leagues: the National Women's Hockey League (NWHL), and the Canadian Women's Hockey League (CWHL), with teams in the United States, Canada, and China. The CWHL first formed in 2007, and the NWHL began play in 2015. It won't be long before those leagues begin writing their own record books. Here are the teams in those upstart leagues:

NWHL

Boston Pride

Metropolitan Riveters

Buffalo Beauts

Minnesota Whitecaps

Connecticut Whale

CWHL

Boston Blades

Markham Thunder

Calgary Inferno

Toronto Furies

Kunlun Red Star (China)

Vanke Rays (China)

Les Canadiennes de Montreal

Read More

Frederick, Shane. *Hockey Is a Number's Game: A Fan's Guide to Stats.* North Mankato, Minn.: Capstone Press, 2018.

Frederick, Shane. *Wacky Hockey Trivia: Fun Facts for Every Fan.* North Mankato, Minn.: Capstone Press, 2017.

Editors of Sports Illustrated. *Sports Illustrated Kids Hockey: Then to Wow!* Time Inc. Books, 2017.

Internet Sites

Use FactHound to find Internet sites related to this book.

Visit *www.facthound.com*

Just type in 9781543554625 and go.

Check out projects, games and lots more at
www.capstonekids.com